Explode The Code® 2nd Edition 2

Essential lessons for phonics mastery

Nancy Hall • Rena Price

The cab skids and slips.

EDUCATORS PUBLISHING SERVICE
Cambridge and Toronto

Cover art: Hugh Price
Text illustrations: Laura Price, Alan Price, Kelly Kennedy

Printed in Mayfield, PA, in February 2022
ISBN 978-0-8388-7802-6

10 11 12 13 14 PAH 25 24 23 22

Lesson 1

◯ it.

cl- fl- bl-	bl- cl- gl-
bl- fl- gl-	fl- cl- bl-
cl- gl- fl-	cl- bl- fl-
cl- gl- fl-	cl- bl- gl-

1

◯ the same word.

clip	club	clap	(clip)
flop	flap	flop	flip
glum	gum	glum	glun
clop	clop	cop	clap
glen	glue	glen	glem
flap	flab	flop	flap
blot	bot	blat	blot

2

Read, copy, and ◯ it.

black **black**			
clip _ _ _ _			
flat _ _ _ _			
clam _ _ _ _			
clap _ _ _ _			
Glen _ _ _ _			
flag _ _ _ _			

3

◯ it.

club or (cub?)	clip or lip?
block or lock?	flat or fat?
flock or clock?	glass or gas?
clap or cap?	black or back?

Match and write it.

| gas | black | ~~lock~~ | clap | flag |
| clip | clam | lap | glass | back |

lock

	cl	(gl) (a) i	(ss) ff	**glass**
	cl	gl o i	p b	
	bl	b u o	ck z	
	cl	fl a i	m ss	
	cl	bl a i	ck p	
	gl	fl a i	b g	
	cl	c o a	ck m	

6

Yes or no?

	Yes	No
Can a black bat dig?	☒	☐
Can a flag flap?	☐	☐
Will a clip get a tan?	☐	☐
Can a flat clam clap?	☐	☐
Can a big clock tick?	☐	☐
Can you tip a glass?	☐	☐
Can a block run?	☐	☐

X it.

The class claps. The glass cuts.	☒ ☐	
The flat clam is sad. The fat clam is glad.	☐ ☐	
Bill sits on a block. Bill sits on a pin.	☐ ☐	
Glen sits on the clock. The clock sits on Glen.	☐ ☐	
The class slips in the mud. The rat sips a glass of mud.	☐ ☐	
The dog wags the flag. The dog has a clip.	☐ ☐	
Mom put a block in the sock. Al puts Mom in the sock.	☐ ☐	

8

Write it.

clip

*For further practice on these blends, see Book 2½, pp. 1–9.

9

Lesson 2

◯ it.

pl- sl- sk-		sl- pl- sk-	
pl- sl- sk-		sl- pl- sk-	
pl- sl- sk-		pl- sk- sl-	
pl- sl- sk-		pl- sl- sk-	

10

◯ the same word.

plum	plun	plum	plam
plop	plog	pop	plop
slot	solt	slot	stol
skim	skin	skim	skum
plan	plun	pan	plan
slim	slim	slin	slam
skid	skib	skip	skid

Read, copy, and ⬭ it.

plum _ _ _ _			
sled _ _ _ _			
plug _ _ _ _			
skip _ _ _ _			
slap _ _ _ _			
lip _ _ _			
skunk _ _ _ _ _			

12

⬭ it.

plus or pass?	plum or Pam?
slap or sap?	skip or sip?
skip or sip?	sled or led?
skid or kid?	plug or Peg?

Match and write it.

skip	sip	plus	lip	plug
plum	skin	slap	sled	skid

_____

_____

_____

_____

_____

_____

_____

_____

	s	sl	o	i	n	p
	sk	sl	i	a	g	p
	sl	l	u	i	p	f
	pl	sl	u	a	n	s
	s	sk	i	e	t	p
	pl	sk	i	e	p	d
	sl	pl	u	a	n	m

Yes or no?

	Yes	No
Can a plum skip?	☐	☐
Will a skunk sip sap?	☐	☐
Is six plus six ten?	☐	☐
Can you slap a big bug?	☐	☐
Can you skip up a hill?	☐	☐
Can a plum kick a man?	☐	☐
Can you slip in a tub?	☐	☐

X it.

Glen has a flag on his sled.	☐	
The sled slams the flag.	☐	
The rug is in the plum.	☐	
The plum is on the bug.	☐	
The fox slams the clam.	☐	
The clam slaps the fox.	☐	
Bill sits on the plum.	☐	
Bill sits on the tack.	☐	
The plug is at the club.	☐	
The bug hit the tub.	☐	
A clip is on the fox skin.	☐	
The slim fox has a clip.	☐	
The skunk sits on the box.	☐	
The box has a plum on it.	☐	

Write it.

18

Lesson 3

it.

cr- gr- dr-	gr- cr- dr-
cr- dr- gr-	cr- dr- gr-
cr- dr- gr-	gr- dr- cr-
dr- cr- gr-	cr- dr- gr-

the same word.

drag	dag	drap	drag
grip	grip	grap	grib
cram	cran	cram	cam
drug	grab	dug	drug
grit	grib	grut	grit
crop	corp	cop	crop
drill	dill	drill	brill

Read, copy, and ◯ it.

drag _ _ _ _			
crib _ _ _ _			
drop _ _ _ _			
cross _ _ _ _ _			
drip _ _ _ _			
grin _ _ _ _			
crab _ _ _ _			

grass   or   gas?

drag   or   rag?

crib   or   rib?

drop   or   Rob?

crab   or   cab?

grip   or   rip?

drip   or   dip?

crack   or   rock?

Match and write it.

crack	drum	drag	grass	gas
drop	grin	dress	crab	cross

_____

_____

_____

_____

_____

_____

_____

_____

	dr gr	e u	ss t	＿＿＿＿＿＿
	dr cr	u o	ss m	＿＿＿＿＿＿
	dr gr	i a	g p	＿＿＿＿＿＿
	gr cr	o a	ck ss	＿＿＿＿＿＿
	gr r	i u	g p	＿＿＿＿＿＿
	gr g	a e	b ss	＿＿＿＿＿＿
	cr dr	o a	b p	＿＿＿＿＿＿

Yes or no?

	Yes	No
Can a crab mop the hut?	☐	☐
Will a clam nap in a crib?	☐	☐
Can a glass crack?	☐	☐
Will Mom grill a dress?	☐	☐
Can you drop a pin in the grass?	☐	☐
Will I grin if I am sad?	☐	☐
Can you hit and tap a drum?	☐	☐

X it.

The gas drips. ☐	
The glass drips. ☐	
The cat drops the gas. ☐	
The glass drops on the cat. ☐	
The dog cuts the grass. ☐	
The dog naps in the grass. ☐	
The crab digs in the mud. ☐	
The crab nips the bug. ☐	
The dress has a rip. ☐	
Glen has a big grip. ☐	
The kid sits on the drum. ☐	
The bat drags a big drum. ☐	
The pet slaps the gum. ☐	
The pet hops up to the sun. ☐	

Write it.

Lesson 4

◯ it. fr- tr- pr-	pr- br- tr-
tr- pr- fr-	tr- br- pr-
br- pr- tr-	tr- br- fr-
pr- fr- br-	pr- tr- fr-

28

⬭ the same word.

trim	trum	trin	trim
bran	bram	bran	ban
prod	pod	prob	prod
Fret	Fred	Fret	Frat
trick	track	trick	tick
brag	bag	brag	drag
frill	fill	frell	frill

Read, copy, and ⬭ it.

trim			
_ _ _ _			
fed			
_ _ _			
trap			
_ _ _ _			
tack			
_ _ _ _			
trot			
_ _ _ _			
frog			
_ _ _ _			
press			
_ _ _ _ _			

track or tack?

trim or Tim?

Fred or fed?

trot or tot?

trip or rip?

Fran or fan?

tap or trap?

tuck or truck?

Match and write it.

Fred	tap	frog	trap	trim
rip	track	press	brick	trot

_____
_____

_____
_____

_____
_____

_____
_____

_____
_____

_____
_____

_____
_____

_____
_____

32

	Spell			Write
	t tr	i u	ss ck	_____
	tr t	o a	g p	_____
	fr tr	a i	m ck	_____
	br pr	e a	ll ss	_____
	tr t	a i	ck p	_____
	t tr	o a	t p	_____
	tr br	i u	ck m	_____

Yes or no?

	Yes	No
Can a fox press a dress?	☐	☐
Is it fun to go on a trip?	☐	☐
Will a frog nap in a crib?	☐	☐
Can a truck trot?	☐	☐
Will a brick rip?	☐	☐
Can you trap a crab?	☐	☐
Will you sit on a track?	☐	☐

X it.

The clam is in the grass.	☐	
The clam can tap a glass.	☐	
The pup trots up the hill.	☐	
The rat slid on the track.	☐	
Ted is on a truck.	☐	
Ted runs on the track.	☐	
The frog slips in the mud.	☐	
The sled sits in the mud.	☐	
Brad trims the box.	☐	
Tim takes a trip.	☐	
Fran drags a big glass.	☐	
The big class drags a fan.	☐	
The pups trip the crab.	☐	
The pups trot on the track.	☐	

Write it.

*For further practice on these blends, see Book 2½, pp. 28–36.

Lesson 5

◯ it.	
sn- / sp- / sm-	sn- / sm- / sp-
sm- / sn- / sp-	sn- / sp- / sm-
sm- / sn- / sp-	sn- / sp- / sm-
sn- / sp- / sm-	sn- / sm- / sp-

snip	snap	sip	snip
snug	smug	snug	snag
spit	stip	spit	spot
spun	spum	span	spun
snap	sap	snap	smap
smog	snug	smug	smog
small	smell	swell	small

Read, copy, and ⬭ it.

spot			
_ _ _ _ _			
sniff			
_ _ _ _ _			
spell			
_ _ _ _ _			
spin			
_ _ _ _ _			
snip			
_ _ _ _ _			
snack			
_ _ _ _ _			
spill			
_ _ _ _ _			

39

snip   or   sip?

spill   or   fill?

sit   or   spit?

snip   or   sniff?

spot   or   pot?

snap   or   nap?

snack   or   sack?

spell   or   sell?

Match and write it.

spot   spell   sell   spit   spin

fill   snip   snack   skip   sniff

41

s	sn	i	a	p m
sm	sp	a e	ll	ff
sp	s	i	o	d t
sn	sp	i	a	n ck
sm	s	i	e	ss ll
sp	p	u	i	ff n
sm	sp	e	i	ll n

Yes or no?

	Yes	No
Can Mom fix a spot?	☐	☐
Can a glass spill?	☐	☐
Can you smell a skunk?	☐	☐
Can a snack grin?	☐	☐
Can a truck spell well?	☐	☐
Can you fill the spots?	☐	☐
Will a top spin and spin?	☐	☐

43

The sled slips.	☐	
The snack skips.	☐	
Ted slaps his skin.	☐	
Ted has spots on his skin.	☐	
The snack smells.	☐	
The snack spills.	☐	
The skunk slid on a sled.	☐	
The skunk sniffs the bud.	☐	
Don spits on the spot.	☐	
Don spills the pot of mud.	☐	
The crab skips and spins.	☐	
The cab skids and slips.	☐	
Jeff can spell well.	☐	
Jeff smells the skunk.	☐	

Write it.

Lesson 6

⬭ it.

sw- tw- st-		st- tw- sw-
st- tw- sw-		sw- tw- st-
sw- tw- st-		tr- sw- st-
sw- tw- st-		tw- st- sw-

46

◯ the same word.

stem	sten	stum	stem
swell	sell	smell	swell
stuff	stiff	stuff	staff
stack	sack	stick	stack
swim	swum	swan	swim
twig	twit	twin	twig
still	stall	still	slit

Read, copy, and ⬭ it.

stem			
_ _ _ _			
swim			
_ _ _ _			
twig			
_ _ _ _			
stop			
_ _ _ _			
stick			
_ _ _ _ _			
stuck			
_ _ _ _ _			
twin			
_ _ _ _			

◯ it.

stem   or   ten?

twin   or   tin?

swim   or   win?

stem   or   sun?

stick   or   sick?

stop   or   top?

twig   or   wig?

stuck   or   suck?

Match and write it.

spin	tack	twig	wig	stop
twin	stem	stuck	step	still

_____

_____

_____

_____

_____

_____

_____

_____

Spell. | Write.

	st sw	i e	m p	_____
	s st	e i	p ck	_____
	sw st	i o	w m	_____
	w tw	a i	g p	_____
	st sw	a u	t ck	_____
	t tw	i e	n g	_____
	st sw	u o	p b	_____

51

Yes or no?

	Yes	No
Can a truck get stuck?	☐	☐
Can you stop on a step?	☐	☐
Will a wet twig swim?	☐	☐
Will I yell if I step in a trap?	☐	☐
Can you stack twigs in a crib?	☐	☐
Can a stick skip up steps?	☐	☐
Can you swim well in a pan?	☐	☐

X it.

Fred has a swell snack. Fred has a stack of bricks.	☐ ☐	
The frog will stop the drip. The cop stops the truck.	☐ ☐	
The twins trip on the tack. The twins hid in the truck.	☐ ☐	
The duck is on a trip. The duck is in a trap.	☐ ☐	
Peg has a stack of sticks. Peg spills a lot of pins.	☐ ☐	
Fred sniffs the swell smell. Fred's skin sticks to a pin.	☐ ☐	
Pam stops on the top step. Pam sits on the steps.	☐ ☐	

Write it.

⬭ it.

flag
fat
flat

clop
clip
clap

sell
spell
smell

drug
drag
drip

cross
press
pass

gas
grass
glass

stack
stuck
stick

slam
slim
Sam

Match and write it.

step	grin	trick	dress	smell
track	twig	flag	clock	snip

_____ - - - - - - - - - _____

_____ - - - - - - - - - _____

_____ - - - - - - - - - _____

_____ - - - - - - - - - _____

_____ - - - - - - - - - _____

_____ - - - - - - - - - _____

_____ - - - - - - - - - _____

Spell.   Write.

sm sk	a i	d n		_____
cr gr	o a	ss ff		_____
cl sl	i a	m ll		_____
dr sl	i u	p m		_____
bl pl	o u	ck t		_____
br pr	a e	t ss		_____
cl br	i o	ck p		_____

57

Yes or no?

	Yes	No
Can a truck skid in the mud?	☐	☐
Will Ben be sad if he is glad?	☐	☐
Can Fred drag a truck?	☐	☐
Can you plan a trip?	☐	☐
Can a drum grin?	☐	☐
Will you grab a clip?	☐	☐
Can you crack a glass if you drop it?	☐	☐

Write it.

*For further practice on these blends, see Book 2½,
pp. 19–27 and 37–45.

59

Lesson 8

Find it at the end as in ma<u>sk</u>.

-st -sk -mp	-st -sk -mp
-st -sk -mp	-sk -mp -st
-st -mp -sk	-sk -mp -st
-mp -st -sk	-st -mp -sk

cast	cask	cats	cast
fast	fact	fats	fast
task	test	task	tusk
must	muts	nust	must
dump	damp	bump	dump
just	jusk	just	juts
past	past	pats	pest

Read, copy, and ⬭ it.

cast _ _ _ _			
last _ _ _ _			
jump _ _ _ _			
vest _ _ _ _			
list _ _ _ _			
fist _ _ _ _			
ask _ _ _			

62

it.

hump or hum?

camp or cap?

cast or cat?

pump or pup?

nest or net?

fist or fit?

lamp or lap?

mask or mass?

Match and write it.

fist	last	lamp	mask	cast
desk	list	hump	dump	jump

	c s	o a	st sk	_____
	n p	e u	st t	_____
	t l	i a	p mp	_____
	h v	u a	m mp	_____
	m w	a i	st sk	_____
	b d	a u	mp m	_____
	d g	u e	sk st	_____

65

Yes or no?

	Yes	No
Can a fast frog jump?	☐	☐
Can you ask a pal to swim?	☐	☐
Can a truck dump logs?	☐	☐
Can you camp on a desk?	☐	☐
Can you plug in a lamp?	☐	☐
If you ran last, did you win?	☐	☐
Will a vest fit a clam?	☐	☐

X it.

The lamp is on the desk. ☐	
The lamp is on the sled. ☐	
The crab has a mask. ☐	
The crab has six mitts. ☐	
The pump is stuck. ☐	
The pup has a snack. ☐	
Fred runs to the camp. ☐	
The pump got Fred wet. ☐	
The desk is on the truck. ☐	
The desk is in the trap. ☐	
A frog jumps to the pad. ☐	
A pup jumps on the frog. ☐	
The truck dumps the bricks. ☐	
The truck bumps the bed. ☐	

Write it.

68

Lesson 9

Find it at the end as in a<u>nt</u>.

-ft -nt -lt		-nt -lt -ft
-sk -lt -ft		-ft -nt -lt
-lt -nt -ft		-ft -lt -nt
-lt -nt -ft		-ft -nt -lt

lift	left	felt	lift
felt	fell	left	felt
went	wet	went	wont
left	lift	left	felt
raft	reft	rat	raft
mint	mitt	mink	mint
wilt	welt	melt	wilt

Read, copy, and ⬭ it.

lift _ _ _ _			
melt _ _ _ _			
hunt _ _ _ _			
sent _ _ _ _			
gift _ _ _ _			
ant _ _ _ _			
raft _ _ _ _			

belt or bell?

lift or lit?

sent or set?

melt or met?

bent or bet?

hunt or hut?

tent or ten?

rat or raft?

Match and write it.

melt ant hunt bent gift	
raft sent belt lift tent	

Spell.   Write.

	b h	a e	nt lt	_____ _____
	t s	i e	n nt	_____ _____
	n m	e a	lt nt	_____ _____
	p g	e i	nt ft	_____ _____
	h n	a u	nt t	_____ _____
	s l	o i	ft t	_____ _____
	r n	i a	ft t	_____ _____

74

Yes or no?

	Yes	No
Can a raft melt?	☐	☐
Can you trap an ant in a net?	☐	☐
Will a clock hunt?	☐	☐
Can a belt jump?	☐	☐
Can you camp in a tent?	☐	☐
Can a gift be sent?	☐	☐
Can you lift a truck of bricks?	☐	☐

X it.

The ant is wet.	☐	
The ant met a pet.	☐	
Glen has a gift of plants.	☐	
Glen has a gift of pans.	☐	
The big tent is wet.	☐	
Big Stan went west.	☐	
The rat has a trap.	☐	
Sam naps on a raft.	☐	
Fran's gift is a big belt.	☐	
Fran's snack will melt and drip.	☐	
Fluff pats the pup.	☐	
Fluff lifts the pump.	☐	
The bed is in the tent.	☐	
The belt will fit ten men.	☐	

Write it.

Lesson 10

Find it at the end as in e<u>lf</u>.

-lf -lp -nd	-nk -nd -lf
-lf -nk -nd	-lf -nk -nd
-lp -nd -nk	-nd -nk -lk
-lp -nk -nd	-nk -nd -nt

$\bigcirc$ the same word.

elf	egg	end	elf
self	silf	sefl	self
pink	pick	pink	pint
end	end	emd	and
sand	send	sand	stand
sink	sunk	sink	stink
hand	band	hind	hand

79

Read, copy, and ⬭ it.

elf — — —			
skunk — — — — —			
wind — — — —			
sand — — — —			
sink — — — —			
band — — — —			
gulp — — — —			

spunk or skunk?

pond or pod?

bend or bed?

wind or win?

wink or win?

band or bend?

hand or had?

ink or in?

Match and write it.

skunk   band   hand   wink   bend

pond   sand   wind   golf   sink

Spell. Write.

	sk sp	e u	nk lt	_____
	sk w	i u	nk nd	_____
	h st	e a	nd lp	_____
	b s	a e	nt nd	_____
	w m	i u	nd nt	_____
	s f	a i	nk nd	_____
	p g	i o	lp lf	_____

83

Yes or no?

	Yes	No
Can an elf wink?	☐	☐
Is golf fun?	☐	☐
Will a hand melt?	☐	☐
Can a sink wink?	☐	☐
Can you send a gift?	☐	☐
Can you dig sand?	☐	☐
Will a pond jump?	☐	☐

X it.

The band is on the raft.	☐	
The band is in bed.	☐	
The big ant sits at the sink.	☐	
The ant lifts the pans.	☐	
Ted jumps in the pond.	☐	
Ted jumps in the pot.	☐	
The dump truck winks.	☐	
The truck sank in the pond.	☐	
The twig bent in the wind.	☐	
The flag flaps in the wind.	☐	
A mask is in his hand.	☐	
A map is in his hand.	☐	
The skunk swims well.	☐	
Fred's tent is a mess.	☐	

Write it.

*For further practice on these blends, see Book 2½, pp. 46–81.

⬭ it.

crest crust crumb	held help hump
skum skunk stump	pans pants plant
track truck trunk	spent swept slept
trust twist twins	sand stand stamp
stand send spend	slept slips steps

Match and write it.

skunk   stamp   drink   swept   milk

trunk   crust   blink   slept   plant

	cr r	u o	st nt	_____
	pl p	u a	mp nts	_____
	s sw	i e	pt ft	_____
	h tr	u e	nk nd	_____
	st sw	a o	nd mp	_____
	p pl	u a	nt nd	_____
	bl dr	u i	nk ft	_____

89

X it.

The truck has a dent. ☐ The trunk has a dent. ☐		
Glen is cross at the crack in the glass. ☐ Glen grins at the clam in the grass. ☐		
Brad slept in his bunk. ☐ Brad slips at the bank. ☐		
Dad sent Mom a plan. ☐ Mom set the plant on Dad. ☐		
Jeff winks at the truck. ☐ Jeff twists the track. ☐		
Fred drinks milk. ☐ Fred will sink the list. ☐		
Fran held the lamp. ☐ The bug lands on Fran. ☐		

Write it.

1.	brick blink drink	2.	cross crest crust
3.	slept swept swift	4.	stand stamp stink
5.	held help honk	6.	drink drift drips
7.	grand grass grant	8.	spill spend slept
9.	trunk trust truck	10.	lift left felt

1.

2.

3.

4.

5.

1. It can jump well. It swims in a pond. It will plop on a pad and sit in the sun and blink. It is a fr_____.

2. It has a stem. It will get big. It will wilt if it is in the hot sun a lot. It is a pl_____.

3. You drink it from a glass. It is fun to sip as a snack, but do not spill it. It is m_____.

4. At camp you run and swim. It is fun! You nap on cots in a t_____.